Montville Township Public Library
90 Horseneck Road
Montville, N.J. 07045-9626
973-402-0900

Library Hours

Monday	9 a.m. - 9 p.m.
Tuesday	9 a.m. - 9 p.m.
Wednesday	9 a.m. - 9 p.m.
Thursday	9 a.m. - 9 p.m.
Friday	9 a.m. - 6 p.m.
Saturday	9 a.m. - 5 p.m.
Sunday	12 a.m. - 5 p.m.

see website www.montvillelibrar.org

GO-KART RACING

BY JOHN HAMILTON

A&D Xtreme
An imprint of Abdo Publishing | www.abdopublishing.com

Visit us at
www.abdopublishing.com

Printed in the United States of America, North Mankato, Minnesota.
052014
092014

 PRINTED ON RECYCLED PAPER

Editor: Sue Hamilton
Graphic Design: John Hamilton
Cover Photo: Corbis
Interior Photos: Corbis, pg. 7, 8-9, 12-13, 16, 20-21, 23, 25 (inset), 28-29, 29 (inset); Getty Images, pg. 4, 18-19; Glow Images, pg. 24-25, 26-27; Thinkstock, pg. 1, 2, 6, 10-11, 14 (inset), 14-15, 17, 22, 30-31, 32.

Websites
To learn more about Action Sports, visit booklinks.abdopublishing.com. These links are routinely monitored and updated to provide the most current information available.

Library of Congress Control Number: 2014932221

Cataloging-in-Publication Data

Hamilton, John.
 Go-kart racing / John Hamilton.
   p. cm. -- (Action sports)
Includes index.
ISBN 978-1-62403-440-4
1. Karting--Juvenile literature.   I. Title.
796.7/6--dc23

2014932221

CONTENTS

THRILLS ON FOUR WHEELS

There's nothing quite as thrilling as kart racing. Go-karts are small, but they pack a big punch. Even karts ridden in amusement parks reach speeds of 15 miles per hour (24 kph) or more. But since riders are mere inches from the ground, the scenery goes by in a blur. Add breakneck acceleration and hyper-responsive handling, and kart racing becomes one of the most exciting motorsports anyone can try, young or old.

Xtreme Fact: Specialized karts on outdoor tracks can hit insane speeds of more than 150 miles per hour (241 kph)!

Kart racing is great training for other kinds of motorsports, such as NASCAR or Formula One racing. Drivers learn the basics of wheel-to-wheel competition, without the costs or dangers of "real" racing. But kart racing is so exciting and competitive that many drivers stay in this class of motorsport. For them, the thrills can't be beat.

British Formula One racing driver Lewis Hamilton teaches a kart driving class in Barcelona, Spain, in 2014. Hamilton was the 2008 Formula One World Champion.

Xtreme Fact: Many Formula One and NASCAR champions, such as Michael Schumacher and Jeff Gordon, got their start racing karts.

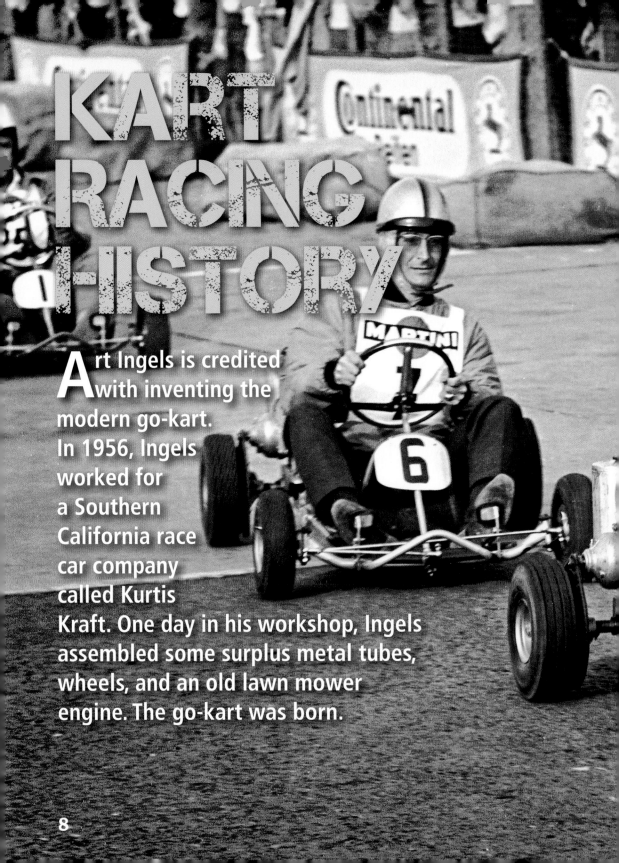

KART RACING HISTORY

Art Ingels is credited with inventing the modern go-kart. In 1956, Ingels worked for a Southern California race car company called Kurtis Kraft. One day in his workshop, Ingels assembled some surplus metal tubes, wheels, and an old lawn mower engine. The go-kart was born.

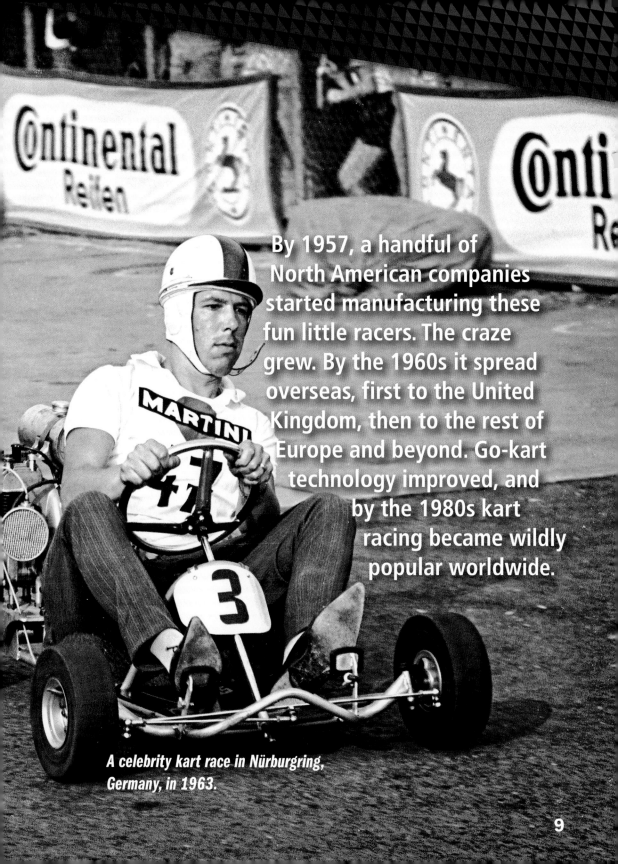

By 1957, a handful of North American companies started manufacturing these fun little racers. The craze grew. By the 1960s it spread overseas, first to the United Kingdom, then to the rest of Europe and beyond. Go-kart technology improved, and by the 1980s kart racing became wildly popular worldwide.

A celebrity kart race in Nürburgring, Germany, in 1963.

WHAT IS A KART?

A go-kart, often simply called a kart, is a small, "open-wheel" vehicle with four wheels. Karts have no suspension, like springs or shock absorbers. The chassis, which is made of steel tubes, is designed to flex to absorb road bumps. Because there is no suspension, drivers sit low to the ground. Karts are very light, eliminating the need for large brakes, tires, and clutches.

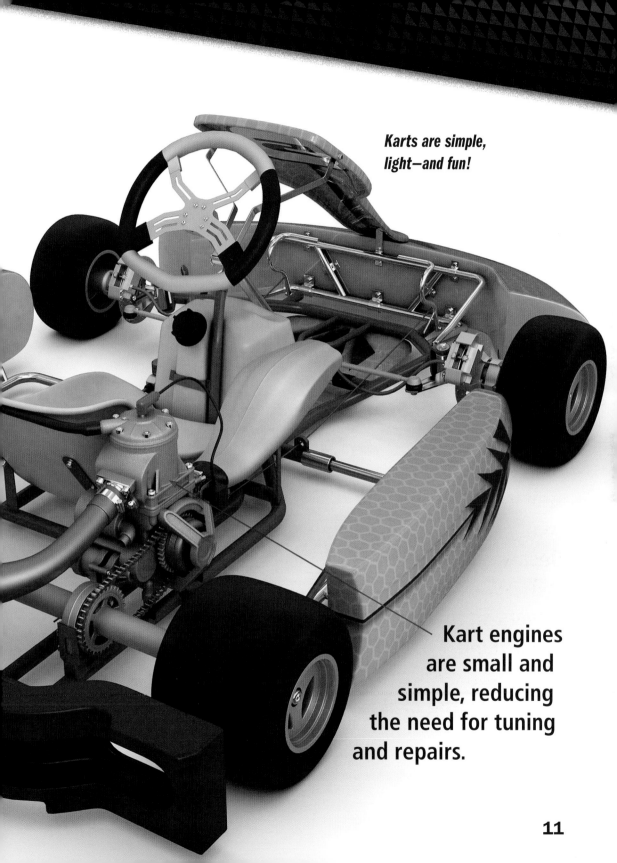

Karts are simple, light—and fun!

Kart engines are small and simple, reducing the need for tuning and repairs.

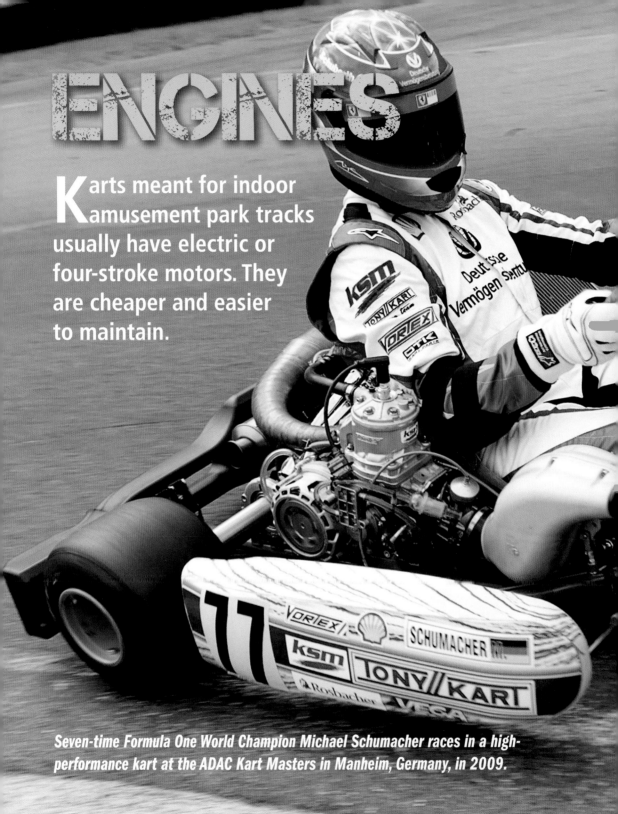

ENGINES

Karts meant for indoor amusement park tracks usually have electric or four-stroke motors. They are cheaper and easier to maintain.

Seven-time Formula One World Champion Michael Schumacher races in a high-performance kart at the ADAC Kart Masters in Manheim, Germany, in 2009.

For serious competition on outdoor tracks, karts use powerful two-stroke engines. Engine size is measured in cubic centimeters. Most kart engines range from about 60 to 250 cc. The most common kart engine size is 125 cc.

TIRES

Kart tires are much smaller than those found on other vehicles. Tires connect the kart to the road. This is very important for sharp turns. If there is not enough traction, the kart skids, and the racer loses valuable time. Tires meant for outdoor tracks are soft. They grip the road very well. Slick tires are meant for dry weather. For rainy weather or dirt tracks, tires have grooves called treads that give more traction.

Tires with treads work well on wet tracks.

Go-kart tires meant for serious racing are smooth and soft, for better track-gripping performance.

SAFETY GEAR

Kart racing is a safe motorsport compared to stock car racing or Formula One. Nevertheless, certain equipment is required for competitive racing. The most important item is a full-face helmet, often called a lid. Helmets should be safety certified and

properly sized. Full driving suits protect the skin in case of crashes or brushing up against other karts. Other protective gear includes gloves, boots, rib protectors, and neck braces.

A young kart racer wearing a helmet and a Nomex fireproof hood.

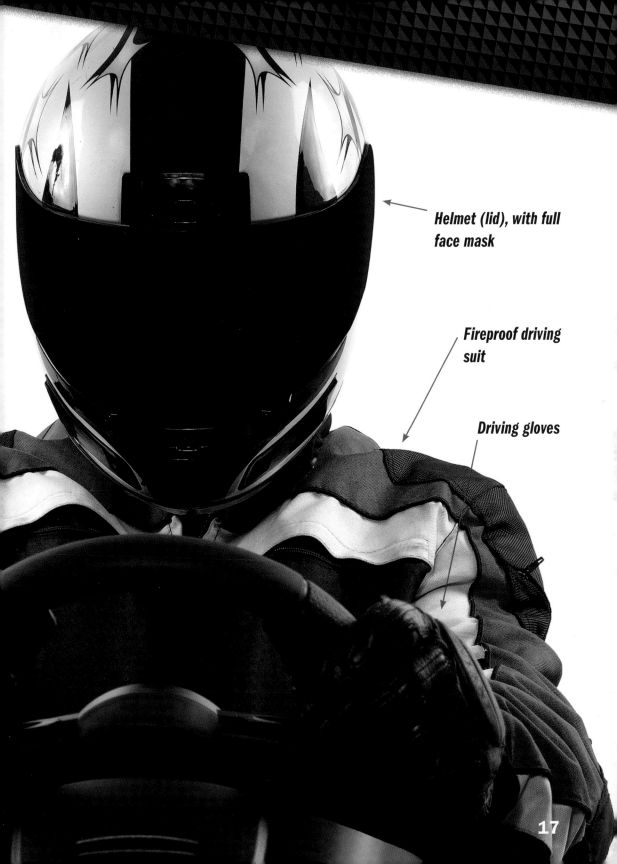

Helmet (lid), with full face mask

Fireproof driving suit

Driving gloves

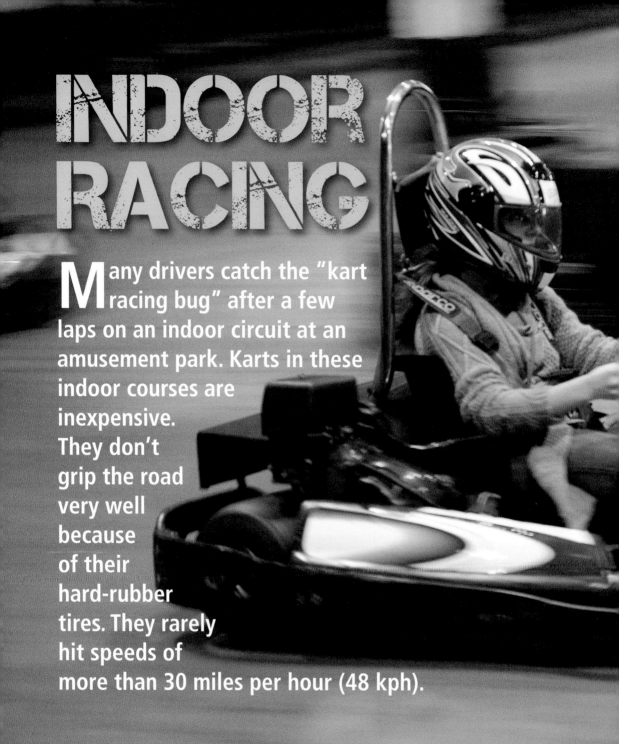

INDOOR RACING

Many drivers catch the "kart racing bug" after a few laps on an indoor circuit at an amusement park. Karts in these indoor courses are inexpensive. They don't grip the road very well because of their hard-rubber tires. They rarely hit speeds of more than 30 miles per hour (48 kph).

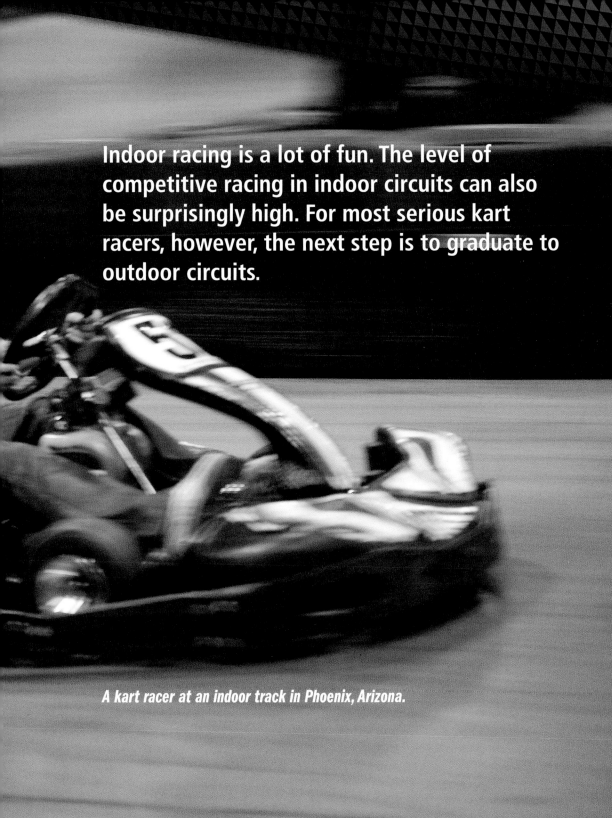

Indoor racing is a lot of fun. The level of competitive racing in indoor circuits can also be surprisingly high. For most serious kart racers, however, the next step is to graduate to outdoor circuits.

A kart racer at an indoor track in Phoenix, Arizona.

OUTDOOR RACING

Most serious kart drivers do their racing on outdoor circuits. The tracks can be either hard asphalt or packed dirt. They can have lots of turns, like a Grand Prix-style track, or they can be simple ovals.

Karts built for outdoor racing are fast. Some can reach speeds of up to 150 miles per hour (241 kph). Most major kart competitions take place on outdoor tracks.

KART CLASSES

Kart racing appeals to all kinds of people, from beginners to professional competitors. There are many kart racing organizations worldwide that divide competition into various skill levels, or classes. In the United States, there are racing classes for kids as young as five years old. In addition to age, classes are also broken down by engine type or manufacturer.

As you get older and your skill level or equipment improves, you can always move up to a higher class for more challenging competition.

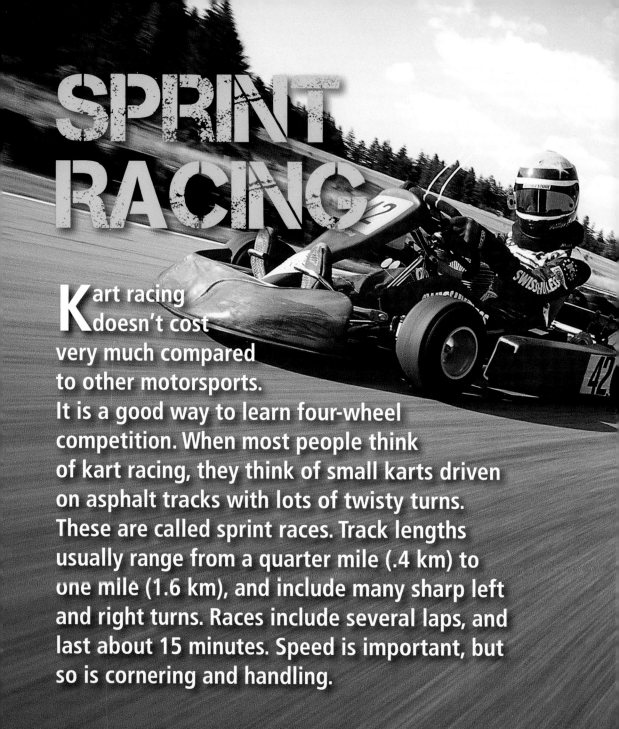

SPRINT RACING

Kart racing doesn't cost very much compared to other motorsports. It is a good way to learn four-wheel competition. When most people think of kart racing, they think of small karts driven on asphalt tracks with lots of twisty turns. These are called sprint races. Track lengths usually range from a quarter mile (.4 km) to one mile (1.6 km), and include many sharp left and right turns. Races include several laps, and last about 15 minutes. Speed is important, but so is cornering and handling.

Sprint racing requires making a lot of turns on twisty tracks. Speed and handling are equally important.

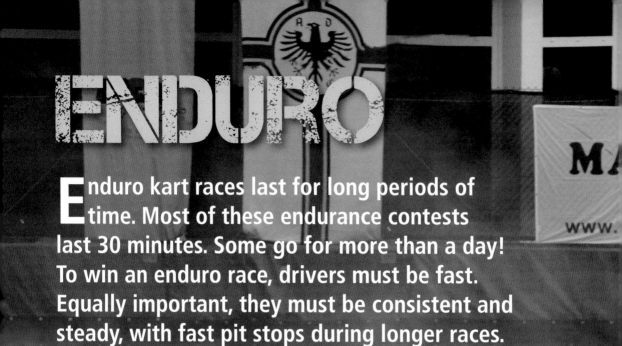

ENDURO

Enduro kart races last for long periods of time. Most of these endurance contests last 30 minutes. Some go for more than a day! To win an enduro race, drivers must be fast. Equally important, they must be consistent and steady, with fast pit stops during longer races.

A professional kart racing championship in Ampfing, Germany.

SPEEDWAY

Speedway racing competition takes place on oval tracks. The tracks are either hard asphalt or packed dirt or clay. Speedway track lengths are usually between 1/6 and 1/4 mile (.27 - .4 km). Racers travel counterclockwise, with left-hand turns only. Many dirt speedway tracks are found in the South and Southeast United States.

Xtreme Fact: Kart racing on speedways is sometimes used as a steppingstone to stock car racing.

No matter what kind of kart racing you prefer, there's nothing quite as thrilling as crossing the finish line in first place.

GLOSSARY

Circuit Racing
A race on a closed track where racers all begin at once.

Formula One
Single-seat, open-wheel racing vehicles, also called F1. They are the fastest circuit-racing cars in the world, reaching speeds of more than 220 miles per hour (354 kph).

Grand Prix
A French phrase meaning "grand prize," it usually refers to Formula One races. They feature hairpin curves and fast straightaways.

NASCAR
The National Association for Stock Car Auto Racing, started in 1948 by race car driver Bill France Sr. Today, NASCAR oversees the largest and most popular racing series in the world.

Open Wheel
Go-karts are open-wheel, meaning their wheels are outside the main body of the vehicle. They are unlike street or sports cars, which have wheels behind fenders.

Pit Stop
When a vehicle halts momentarily in a special maintenance area. Mechanics quickly perform work such as refueling or changing tires.

Stock Car
Race cars bought from dealer "stock" and modified to make them lighter and more powerful.

INDEX